2021

LONDON

Restaurants

The Food Enthusiast's

Long Weekend Guide

Andrew Delaplaine

D1593826

Andrew Delaplaine is the Food Enthusiast.

When he's not playing tennis,

he dines anonymously

at the Publisher's (sometimes considerable) expense.

WANT 3 FREE THRILLERS?

Why, of course you do!
If you like these writers--
Vince Flynn, Brad Thor, Tom Clancy, James Patterson,
David Baldacci, John Grisham, Brad Meltzer, Daniel
Silva, Don DeLillo
If you like these TV series –
House of Cards, Scandal, West Wing, The Good Wife,
Madam Secretary, Designated Survivor

You'll love the **unputdownable** series about
Jack Houston St. Clair, with political intrigue, romance,
and loads of action and suspense.

Besides writing travel books, I've written political thrillers
for many years that have delighted hundreds of thousands
of readers. I want to introduce you to my work!
Send me an email and I'll send you a link where you can
download the first 3 books in my bestselling series,
absolutely FREE.
Mention **this book** when you email me.

The Food Enthusiast's Complete Restaurant Guide

Table of Contents

Introduction – 5

Getting About – 7

The A to Z Listings – 19
Ridiculously Extravagant
Sensible Alternatives
Quality Bargain Spots

Nightlife – 97

Index – 107

Other Books by the Food Enthusiast – 112

INTRODUCTION

I kept a place in London for many years, in West Kensington near Notting Hill, but have lived there off and on since then. I've probably spent more time in London than any other city, and while it's a toss-up whether I prefer New York to London, the fact of the matter is I lived in London longer than New York, so that pretty much tells you.

"Why, Sir, you find no man, at all intellectual, who is willing to leave London. No, Sir, when a man is tired of London, he is tired of life; for there is in London all that life can afford."

Samuel Johnson said this to James Boswell when they were discussing whether or not Boswell's affection for London would wear thin should he choose to live there, as opposed to the zest he felt on his occasional visits. (Boswell lived in Scotland, and visited only periodically. Some people are surprised to learn that Boswell and Johnson were far from inseparable over the last twenty years of Johnson's life, the period Boswell knew him.)

This discussion happened on September 20, 1777, and Johnson, who had an unusual fear of being alone, was always going out and enjoying what London had to offer. I couldn't agree more wholeheartedly with Johnson, and his observation of the London of 1777 is just as apt today.

GETTING ABOUT

THE UNDERGROUND
People have been using the Underground, more commonly known as the Tube, since 1863. This is a public metro system that serves a large part of Greater London as well as parts of the counties of Buckinghamshire, Hertfordshire and Essex. The Underground has 270 stations.

While it's possibly the best means of transportation when considering area covered, speed and reliability, there are a few disadvantages. In the summer it's hot and crowded and is not a place you want to be stuck on a summer's day and it's become a bit pricey for visitors to use. While I used to use the Tube quite often when I lived in London during most of the 1980s, I don't use it as much when I'm on short visits, preferring the speediness and comfort of taxis. I also prefer the bus to the Tube.

If you are planning on using the Tube, you should plan your journey and try to avoid rush hour. Check out the Journey Planner on the Transport for London website - www.tfl.gov.uk - where you will find the quickest route to your destination. Check the notice boards at each station for travel information, delays and updates. Wait until those leaving the train have exited before getting on. Always check your ticket and make sure that you have purchased the correct ticket for your destination and that it covers all zones that you will be traveling through. Make sure that you are going to the correct platform as many stations have multiple platforms. (Example: Euston station has six platforms for two underground lines.)

Greater London is served by 12 Tube lines that run between 5 a.m. and midnight, Monday to Saturday, with reduced operating hours on Sunday. Fares vary depending on times and zones so if you're traveling on the Tube you should consider purchasing an **Oyster Card** or a **Travelcard** to get the best fares and not have to stand in the lines. (Note: You don't want to be caught on the Tube without a valid ticket because you're liable for an immediate fine.) Pick up a London Underground map at any London Tube station or a London Travel Information center.

S

TAXIS

A visit to London is not complete without a ride in one of the city's black cabs, the official cabs of London. These iconic symbols of London, with their unusual round shape, were originally designed to comfortably transport a gentleman wearing a bowler hat. The cabs may be hailed on the street or booked in advance for door-to-door service. Cabs have yellow TAXI sign on the roof of the vehicle and when illuminated the cab is available.

Only hail a cab on the street if you are not near a "rank," the term Londoners use for their cabstands. At a rank, cabs and passengers line up allowing the first in line to be served. Black cabs can be booked in

advance by phone or online at
www.londonblackcabs.co.uk

Unlike many US cab drivers, London cab drivers are quite knowledgeable. In fact, I think they're the best cabbies in the whole world.

Potential cabbies must pass an exam that requires them to have extensive knowledge of London including memorizing over 25,000 streets and 320 routes so when you travel by cab, your driver is not only an excellent source of information, be assured you won't get lost and will get to your destination by the best route available. Black cabs can accommodate up to five passengers, including luggage, at no extra charge. All cabs are wheelchair accessible and guide dogs ride for free. Tipping isn't required but is expected.

MINICABS

Minicabs are not available on the street and must be booked in advance. Most hotels and hostels will have a list of reputable and licensed cab operators. Minicab drivers do not have the vast knowledge required of black cab drivers so they are not experts on streets and routes. The advantage to taking a minicab is the price. While they are cheaper than black cabs, you must negotiate the price when booking your ride. Beware: there are minicabs that will offer you rides on the street at cheaper rates but realize that these are unlicensed cabs and you do not want to get into an unlawful vehicle.

BUSES

One of the best ways to see London is on the famous red double-decker buses. The red buses offer great sightseeing opportunities while you're getting around London. London boasts one of the largest networks of buses with approximately 7,500 iconic red buses. These buses travel all over London with 19,500 bus stops and stations. There is a flat fare throughout the bus network but the fares are cheaper with a pre-paid Oyster Card. Travelcards are accepted on all buses. Most buses require you to buy tickets before you board so you must purchase tickets at the machines located next to the main bus stops. London buses run all night so bus service is available after the Tube closes. Check bus-stop information boards for route info. For more information on routes and schedules visit these sites: www.tfl.gov.uk or www.londonbusroutes.net

BY CAR

London has an excellent public transportation system which makes it the quickest way to get about. I definitely recommend you NOT drive in London for several reasons.

One, many are not used to the fact that the British drive on the "wrong side" of the road and the driver sits on the right side of the car. This in itself takes a bit of readjustment and can be tricky particularly at peak times. Most cars are manual transmission and that's what you'll be given at any rental company unless you make a reservation for an automatic. Drivers must abide by all the rules of London and all drivers must wear seatbelts. It is also very difficult to find parking space in London and parking can be very expensive. A non-UK driving license is valid in Britain for up to 12 months from the date of your last entry. For full details of the legal requirements for drivers visit the Department for Transport website: www.tfl.gov.uk.

BY BICYCLE

Seeing London by bike is not only great exercise but also an economic way to explore the city. Visit the Transport for London website for cycle routes - www.tfl.gov.uk All bikers must wear helmets. There are several companies that rent mountain or hybrid bikes – deposits are required. **The London Bicycle Tour Company** (www.londonbicycle.com) rents bikes at reasonable rates and offers daily bike tours of London. Another way to rent bikes is through **Barclays Cycle Hire**, called Boris Bikes after Boris who was mayor of London when the project was launched, which has more than 8,000 bikes and over 550 bike docking stations around the city. The system is fairly easy, just hire a bike, ride it, then return it at any docking station. Bikers need a debit or credit card to register. Folding bikes are allowed on all Tube lines, river services, local trains, the Docklands Light Railway and London's Tramlink without restrictions.

MOTORBIKES AND SCOOTERS

If you're going to travel the streets of London by motorbike or scooter be aware of all driving rules and remember that you're driving on the other side of the street. Bikers must wear helmets. Also note that many of the roads are narrow, busy and congested even during non-peak driving times. There are benefits to riding a motorbike or scooter in London and many commuters choose bikes over cars. With a motorbike you can travel through traffic faster, avoid public transportation, and it's easier to find parking. There are several outlets offering rentals such as Motorcyle**Hire**Uk www.superbikerental.co.uk.

GETTING TO AND FROM THE AIRPORT

HEATHROW AIRPORT

Heathrow Airport, located to the west of Central London, handles more international passengers than any other airport in the world. With 5 busy terminals filled with a variety of shops, restaurants, information counters, and exchange facilities, this airport can seem a maze with its crowds of incoming and outgoing passengers. All arrivals can be found on the ground floor of Terminals 1, 3, 4 and 5. All arrivals must go through passport control, baggage reclaim and Customs. Departures can be found on the first floor of Terminals 1 and 2, the ground floor of Terminal 3 and the top floor of Terminal 5. Remember that all passengers must first go through security control before entering the departure lounge. Always double check the Heathrow website to confirm your terminal.

Traveling by Car

Heathrow is located approximately 17 miles west of central London. If you're traveling by car, most of the trip can be made via the M4 motorway but avoid traveling during peak periods as it can get congested. The airport is also near the M40 and M3 and Terminal 5 can be reached directly from the M25. There are ample parking facilities at Heathrow; however, each car park has their own rules and rates.

Car rental centers are located along the northern edge of the airport with free shuttle buses available from all terminals. Beware of the long lines at the hire desks (satellite rental services) and if you arrive during early morning or late evening you may have to take a shuttle bus and check out your rental at the depot. If you are driving to the center of London be warned that you will be liable for the Congestion Charge (£8 per day during weekdays between 7am-6pm). Note that automatic number plate recognition cameras are actively looking for violators and your car rental company will bill you with the £30 fine if you fail to pay.

Public Transportation

London's public transportation system is very good and most of the travelers heading to Central London use public transportation. All Heathrow terminals have public transport links to and from Central London including buses, rail services and London Underground. Heathrow has five different rail stations for the five terminals so make sure that you take the right train as not all trains got to the same terminals. www.**tfl**.gov.uk

By Rail
Trains are a comfortable way to travel to and from the airport as they are quite modern with air-conditioning and Free Wi-Fi access on board. The Heathrow express is the fastest way to travel from Central London to Heathrow and back. The express departs from Terminal 5 every 15 minutes and makes stops at Terminals 1 & 3 then runs non-stop to London Paddington, Central London. The traveling time is approximately 15 minutes. Trains run from Heathrow from 5:42 a.m. until 11:42 p.m. Check the website for schedule and rates.
www.heathrowexpress.com

By London Underground
The most economical way to travel to Heathrow Airport from London is London Underground's Piccadilly Line. Travel time is less than an hour and

the wait time is never more than ten minutes. Heathrow has three London Underground stations: one for Terminals 1 and 3 and one each for Terminal 4 and Terminal 5. All stations are in Travelcard Zone 6. Fares vary depending on how you pay and it's recommended that travelers use Oyster and Travelcards. Remember that the Tube is a rapid transit system designed with short journeys in mind and if you're traveling with luggage this may not be the most comfortable choice. Almost all the stations involve negotiating staircases and escalators. www.tfl.gov.uk

By Bus

The N9, the night bus, runs approximately between the hours of 11:59 p.m. and 5 a.m. This bus runs every 20 minutes to Central London (Trafalgar Square). Travel time is approximately 75 minutes. Standard fares apply and the Oyster Card is accepted. www.tfl.gov.uk

By Taxi

Traveling to Heathrow from London by black cab is easy as the cabbies have extensive knowledge of the terminal. Just book a cab in London, making sure they are aware of your departure time, and your journey will be carefree. Arrivals landing in Heathrow should take note that there are plenty of taxis lined up for customers. Only use a black cab or a reputable minicab. Never use unauthorized drivers. All Heathrow Terminals have an approved taxi desk and stand where taxis can be booked.

THE
A TO Z LISTINGS

Ridiculously Extravagant
Sensible Alternatives
Quality Bargain Spots

10 GREEK STREET
10 Greek St, London, +44 20 7734 4677
www.10greekstreet.com

CUISINE: Modern European
DRINKS: Full Bar
SERVING: Lunch, Dinner
PRICE RANGE: $$$
NEIGHBORHOOD: Bloomsbury
This small eatery offers a small seasonal menu with dishes like Filet of Halibut and Brecon Lamb cutlets. Menu favorite was the Scallops and chorizo. Cocktail list includes several variations on the negroni. Nice wine selection. Tables placed very close together. No reservations. Closed Sundays.

ALAIN DUCASSE AT THE DORCHESTER
Park Lane, Mayfair, 020-7629-8866
www.alainducasse-dorchester.com
CUISINE: French
DRINKS: Full Bar
SERVING: Lunch, Dinner

PRICE RANGE: $$$
NEIGHBORHOOD: Mayfair
This is a lavish restaurant serving French haute cuisine in the luxurious setting of one of London's finest hotels. You feel a little like a titled aristocrat just walking through the lobby. Well, I do, anyway. More Michelin stars have been given to Ducasse than almost any other chef, and he certainly deserves every one of them. Though the hotel is ornate and elaborate, the restaurant itself is quite modern with an entirely contemporary vibe. The jewel of the restaurant is the stunning 'Table Lumière'—this is a semi-private room surrounded by 4,500 shimmering fiber optics dropping dramatically from the ceiling. This is like an expensive shower curtain, to put it bluntly, and encircles the round table where a handful of customers are then secluded from the rest of the room, except that they are right in the middle of it and you can see partially through this moving, living curtain of light. The table is set with Hermès china, gorgeous flatware and Saint-Louis crystal. I find the effect of this table to be a little tacky. The fact that it's in the middle of the room and so completely emphasized is what turns me off. It's as if you're in coach class if you're on this side of the barrier and whoever's on the other side of that glittering curtain is in first class. Not that I didn't want to join them, mind you. Favorites: Pasta cannelloni, the turbot with green almonds and Seared Foie Gras. This is very upscale dining with a dress code. Book ahead.

THE ANCHOR & HOPE
36 The Cut, London, +44 20 7928 9898

www.anchorandhopepub.co.uk
CUISINE: British cuisine
DRINKS: Full Bar
SERVING: Lunch & Dinner
PRICE RANGE: $$
NEIGHBORHOOD: Southwark, Waterloo
Gastropub with an ever-changing menu of modern British fare. The good thing is this place is always packed because the vibe is so cool and the food so good. The bad thing: this place is always packed. Favorites: Dover sole and Lamb shoulder. Try the Poppyseed cheesecake for dessert. You can eat in the dining room or in the bar.

Angler outdoor seating

ANGLER
3 South Place, Finsbury, 020-3215-1250
www.anglerrestaurant.com
CUISINE: British (Modern)
DRINKS: Full Bar
SERVING: Lunch, Dinner
PRICE RANGE: $$$$
NEIGHBORHOOD: Finsbury
Elegant eatery located seven floors up with a seafood-focused menu. This is a popular foodie place and boasts not only a Michelin star, but a killer rooftop terrace with spectacular views. Favorites: Cured sea bass and Roast Newlyn cod. Vegetarian friendly. Impressive wine list with over 250 labels. Incredible views. Reservations recommended.

Angler

AULIS
16-a St Anne's Ct, Soho, 020-3948-9665
www.aulis.london
CUISINE: European / British cuisine
DRINKS: Full Bar
SERVING: Lunch, Dinner
PRICE RANGE: $$$$
NEIGHBORHOOD: Soho
Popular among foodies, this eatery offers the ultimate, interactive dining experience in a little hole in the wall you'll love. It's pretty exclusive dining with only eight seats available. All dishes are cooked in front of you because there's no room to do it anywhere else, the place is so small, and everything is carefully explained, sometimes in excruciating detail. The staff here are so serious, one wants to tell them to lighten up, but they are committed. The menu is ever-changing, and it really matters not what they serve. It's always beyond excellent. Be sure to opt for the wine pairings that are offered. Reservations only

(book way ahead). This is owned by the same team behind **ROGANIC**, and they do a lot of experimenting on dishes here. It's rather difficult to get into, as you can imagine, but well worth a try.

BAO FITZROVIA
31 Windmill St, London, +44 4420 3011 1632
www.baolondon.com
CUISINE: Taiwanese
DRINKS: Full Bar
SERVING: Lunch & Dinner; Closed Sundays
PRICE RANGE: $$
NEIGHBORHOOD: Fitzrovia
Popular hip multi-level eatery in a townhouse in Central London serving creative Taiwanese dishes. They've updated the interiors, so the place is sleek, modern, airy. Their specialty is Ping Paan small platters as well as much bigger platters you can share. Whatever else you order, you must start with a couple of the 'gua baos.' These are little ever-so-fluffy

steamed milk bao buns that are gone in two (or sometimes one) bite. They started off with a street stall and grew into this. Grab a seat at the bar. The waiters will give you a little form. You check off the items you want. (You can add to this later if you want more.) Upstairs is the bar area, while downstairs is the bigger dining room, set with communal tables, a big open kitchen. Favorites: Fried Chicken Chop and Classic Bao. Impressive cocktail selection, but lots of sakes. Dessert: get a bao version of a donut—filled with ice cream. You've never had this before, I'll bet.

BARBARY
16 Neal's Yard, Seven Dials, London, **no phone**
www.thebarbary.co.uk
CUISINE: Middle Eastern / Mediterranean
DRINKS: Full Bar

SERVING: Lunch & Dinner
PRICE RANGE: $$$
NEIGHBORHOOD: Covent Garden
Small eatery (24 numbered seats at the horseshoe-shaped bar where all the action occurs) with a menu of small plates. Focus is cooking with fire, either grilling over coals or baked in clay ovens the way they used to do it hundreds of years ago. (OK, thousands of years ago.) Very hip little place. The music is electro-pop, but not so loud you can't talk. Good alone or for a couple. A party of 4 makes it tough. You wait at a drink rail for your number to come up, but you can order drinks and snacks while you wait. When you get to a bar stool, ask your neighbors what they ordered and try something new and different. You'll be glad you did. Favorites: Arayes (pita pouches grilled and stuffed with seasoned beef & lamb—you'll scarf these down); Cauliflower Jaffa; Lamb Cutlets with cumin crust; Pata Negra neck (pork). Extensive wine list.

BARRAFINA

43 Drury Lane, Covent Garden, +44 20 7440 1456
10 Adelaide St, Covent Garden
26-27 Dean St, Soho
www.barrafina.co.uk
CUISINE: Spanish
DRINKS: Full Bar
SERVING: Lunch, Dinner
PRICE RANGE: $$$
NEIGHBORHOOD: Covent Garden
This popular Spanish eatery in 3 locations offers a
delicious assortment of Mallorcan and Barcelona
style tapas and other Spanish dishes. Menu favorites
include: Grilled chicken thighs with romesco sauce
and Coca Mallorquina. Nice selection of wines by the
glass. Reservations not accepted so expect a wait.
Don't go after 2 p.m. for lunch or you won't get
served.

BEA'S OF BLOOMSBURY

44 Theobalds Rd, London, +44 20 7242 8330
www.beas.london
CUISINE: Bakery
DRINKS: No Booze
SERVING: Tea, Sweets
PRICE RANGE: $$
NEIGHBORHOOD: Bloomsbury

This café is known for its cakes, cupcakes and assorted sweets. This is a great place to come for afternoon tea or something sweet like a scone or a brownie. Other locations in St Paul's and Farringdon.

BENARES

12a Berkeley Square House
Berkeley Square, 020-7629-8866
www.benaresrestaurant.com
CUISINE: Indian
DRINKS: Full Bar
SERVING: Lunch, Dinner
PRICE RANGE: $$$$
NEIGHBORHOOD: Mayfair

This is an upscale eatery serving Indian-British fusion cuisine. Here you'll find Indian cuisine elevated to the Michelin star level. Utterly exquisite food prepared and served impeccably. You can choose from a pre-theatre prix fixe menu or large plates suitable for sharing or opt for the a la carte menu, which is very comprehensive. Favorites: Lamb cutlets with a lovely spiced rub; and Chargrilled Scottish Salmon with lemongrass couscous. There's a daily special menu that's well worth a glance, and a Vegetarian menu is offered as well. Extensive wine list. Creative cocktails like the zingy Passion Fruit

Chutney martini. I know how awful that sounds, but try it, you'll like it. Reservations recommended.

BLACK AXE MANGAL
156 Canonbury St, London, **no phone**
www.blackaxemangal.com
CUISINE: Turkish
DRINKS: Full Bar
SERVING: Dinner Mon – Sat, Brunch Sat & Sun.
PRICE RANGE: $$
NEIGHBORHOOD: Islington
Small simple eatery offering a menu of Turkish-inspired dishes. It's a tiny place that seems even smaller because of the heavy metal music blasting away. Nothing "romantic" about this place, but it is fun. Staff is hip, youngish, tats and t-shirts, and you can tell they *like* this music. A few small tables, but try to snag a seat at the bar where you watch a master at work pulling food from the "mangal grill." Favorites: Lamb offal flatbread; Rabbit in a crispy breading; and Bone marrow flatbread. Nice selection of ales. They take reservations.

BRAWN

49 Columbia Rd, London, +44 20 7729 5692
www.brawn.co
CUISINE: Modern European
DRINKS: Full Bar
SERVING: Lunch, Dinner
PRICE RANGE: $$$
NEIGHBORHOOD: Shoreditch
Lovely restaurant - ideal setting for a date night.
Popular eatery on Columbia Road (widely known for
its flower market on Sunday) offering Mediterranean
small plates menu. They're focused on using local
products whenever possible, like pork belly from
Suffolk. The menu is quite impressive with choices
like Mozzarella & Ratatouille, and Cheese Souffle.
And of course their famous selection of meats.
Tiramisu fans will delight at the giant squares of
tiramisu served for dessert. Serious wine list.
Reservations recommended. Other Favorites: Squid &
black pudding and Oxtail. Good house wine and wine
list. (The wines are mostly all natural.) Menu changes
nightly.

BRIGHT

1 Westgate St, London, +44 20 3095 9407
www.brightrestaurant.co.uk
CUISINE: Italian
DRINKS: Wine
SERVING: Dinner, Lunch & Dinner Fri – Sat;
Closed Mondays
PRICE RANGE: $$$
NEIGHBORHOOD: London Fields

Industrial-style eatery in out-of-the-way London Fields offering sharable seasonal Italian fare. Very much a locals place. Dim candle lighting at night

Bright during the day – it gets romantic at night.

makes the place a nice romantic spot for a date. Menu changes daily (and is date-stamped to prove it), but focuses on comfort food expertly prepared with stellar ingredients. Vegetarian friendly. Favorites: Gnocchetti & pork sausage Campidanese; Steamed chalk stream trout. Impressive wine selection.

BUBBLEDOGS
70 Charlotte St, London, +44 20 7637 7770
www.bubbledogs.co.uk
CUISINE: Hot Dogs, Champagne Bar
DRINKS: Full Bar
SERVING: Lunch, Dinner
PRICE RANGE: $$$
NEIGHBORHOOD: Fitzrovia

A unique concept in Champagne bars, here you'll find hot dogs instead of caviar. The hot dogs are gourmet and there are more tasting samplings on the menu like Crispy Chicken Skin. Hot dog varieties include: Sloppy Joe Dog and Rueben Beef Hot Dog. The Champagne list is also impressive. Oh, there's a speakeasy style room behind this place ((it's screened off with a curtain) that seats 15 to 20. Called the **Kitchen Table**, it offers unique dishes during a 12 to 15 course menu that might include items like ox-heart tartare or chicken skin served with bacon jam. (You'll have to book far in advance, however.)

CAT & MUTTON
76 Broadway Market, London, +44 20 7249 6555
www.catandmutton.com
CUISINE: British cuisine
DRINKS: Full Bar
SERVING: Lunch & Dinner
PRICE RANGE: $$
NEIGHBORHOOD: Broadway Market, London Fields
Traditional gastropub with daily specials and weekend DJ sessions. Favorites: Lamb shoulder and Beer battered Haddock & chips. Nice selection of beers on tap (16) and in bottle (20). Sunday roasts are popular serving excellent Bloody Mary's. Wednesday night is quiz night.

CEVICHE PERUVIAN KITCHEN & PISCO BAR

17 Frith St, London, +44 20 7292 2040
www.cevicheuk.com
CUISINE: Peruvian
DRINKS: Full Bar
SERVING: Lunch, Dinner
PRICE RANGE: $$$
NEIGHBORHOOD: Soho
This tiny restaurant serves authentic Peruvian dishes and fresh ceviche. Menu favorites include: Quinoa Salad and Peruvian Corn Cake. Ceviche is made right in front of you at the Ceviche Bar so you know it's fresh. Ceviche also serves delicious signature cocktails and a nice selection of creative desserts.

CHILTERN FIREHOUSE

1 Chiltern St, London, +44 20 7073 7676
www.chilternfirehouse.com
CUISINE: British; European

DRINKS: Full Bar
SERVING: Breakfast, Lunch, Dinner
PRICE RANGE: $$$
NEIGHBORHOOD: Marlybone
There's counter service, high-top tables, cozy booths if you want privacy, in this brightly decorated spot at the Chiltern with an open kitchen that lets you see the cooks at work. The Chiltern was one of the first purpose-built firehouses in London, and dates back to 1889. Andre Balazs converted it into 26 exquisitely furnished rooms served by a staff trained to pamper you. You will fall in love when you first walk into the cozy lobby. Go for the Vichyssoise with razor clam, Grilled Welsh Lamb Rump with collard greens, Wild Turbot Crudo. Menu changes weekly.

THE CORAL ROOM
Bloomsbury Hotel
16-22 Great Russell St, Bloomsbury, London, +44 20 7347 1221
www.thecoralroom.co.uk
CUISINE: British cuisine
DRINKS: Full Bar
SERVING: Lunch, Dinner
PRICE RANGE: $$$
NEIGHBORHOOD: Bloomsbury
Beautiful lobby bar located in the hotel offering an elegant country house décor. Great cocktails but also an elegant setting for breakfast, coffee or light snack (like the Dorset crab on toast). Live music most evenings.

CLAUDE BOSI AT BIBENDUM
Michelin House, 81 Fulham Rd, 020-7581-5817
http://bibendum.co.uk
CUISINE: French (Modern)
DRINKS: Full Bar
SERVING: Lunch, Dinner
PRICE RANGE: $$$
NEIGHBORHOOD: Chelsea
This is yet another upscale eatery, but this one's on
two levels offering two distinct dining experiences.
On the ground floor is a seafood and oyster bar and
on the floor above you find French Haute Cuisine.
You'll be very impressed with the floor-to-ceiling
stained glass windows offering great views of the

busy streets outside. Menu picks: Cornish Turbot and Line-caught Cornish Cod.

THE CLOVE CLUB
380 Old St, London, 020-7729-6496
https://thecloveclub.com
CUISINE: British
DRINKS: Full Bar
SERVING: Lunch, Dinner

PRICE RANGE: $$$
NEIGHBORHOOD: Shoreditch
Set in the glamorous former Shoreditch Town Hall, this upscale eatery features a seafood focused menu that emphasizes seasonal produce that comes from all parts of the country. Though the setting is slightly informal, there's nothing informal about the high level quality of their Michelin-starred food. Favorites: Scottish Spider Crab Hot Pot and Raw Orkney Scallop, which has become their signature dish. The scallops come from the Orkney Islands off the northeastern coast of Scotland. (Very nippy weather up in these parts, I can tell you from first-hand experience when I spent a bit of time up there drinking whiskey day in and day out. It's so cold up there it's no wonder the Scots drink so much. But I'm forever thankful to the Scots for drowning me in their fabulous spirits.) This dish—I'm back to the scallops—is prepared with Perigord truffles, hazelnuts and clementine or mandarin—unbelievable flavors. You'll get to choose from different prix fixe tasting menus. Any and all are fine in what's come to be known as one of the best restaurants in the world. Impressive wine and cocktail list. Book ahead.

CORA PEARL

30 Henrietta St, Covent Garden, 020-7324-7722
www.corapearl.co.uk
CUISINE: European / British cuisine
DRINKS: Full Bar
SERVING: Lunch, Dinner
PRICE RANGE: $$$
NEIGHBORHOOD: Covent Garden
Located in a chic Convent Garden townhouse, the
menu focus is comfort food elevated to a new level.
Favorites: Fish Stew & Croutons and Tamworth Pork
Chop, with Celeriac & Bordelaise. You have to try
the French fries here, unlike any you've had before.
They are cut thick and look a little stumpy, but the
flavor is out of this world. Book ahead. This is a
perfect choice for pre-theatre dinner. Oh, you might
be interested in the name Cora Pearl. It's well worth
reading the Wikipedia entry on this woman, which I
did on my iPhone when I made my first visit here—
she was a famed Parisian prostitute who reached the

height of her fame as a courtesan in the 1860s. She wasn't French at all, but English, born Eliza Emma Crouch but had a fascinating career once she realized what she was cut out for. I meant to ask why they named this restaurant after the woman, but I was so taken by the food and wine and the fun-loving crowd that I completely forgot.

CORE BY CLAIRE SMYTH
92 Kensington Park Rd, Notting Hill, 020-3937-5086
www.corebyclaresmyth.com
CUISINE: French / European / British
DRINKS: Full Bar
SERVING: Lunch, Dinner
PRICE RANGE: $$$$
NEIGHBORHOOD: Notting Hill
Fine dining in a comfortable setting. British food served at its best, but I found quite a few European influences on this menu, most of them French. The

chef here is the first and only, I might add, female chef to win 3 stars from the folks over at Michelin. As you can see, she's quite celebrated. The décor is sleek, modern, with clean lines and flattering lighting. There's a lovely bar where you can sample some of their creative craft cocktails made to exacting standards. Favorites: Isle of Mull Scallop Tartare and Roasted Monkfish. Vegetarian, Vegan and gluten-free options. Reservations recommended.

CUT
45 Park Lane, London, +44 20 7493 4545
www.45parklane.com
CUISINE: American / Steakhouse
DRINKS: Full Bar
SERVING: Brunch, Lunch, Dinner
PRICE RANGE: $$$
NEIGHBORHOOD: Mayfair
This restaurant is the European debut of chef and restaurateur Wolfgang Puck with a menu that reflects the award winning Beverly Hills counterpart. A simple menu features signature prime steaks and fresh

seafood along with Puck's version of American classics. Classic cocktails and a well crafted wine list. Dining room seats 70 with Bar 45 seating 30.

DARJEELING EXPRESS
Top Floor, Kingly Court, London, +44 20 7287 2828
www.darjeeling-express.com
CUISINE: Indian
DRINKS: Full bar
SERVING: Lunch & Dinner, Lunch only on Sundays; closed Mon & Tues
PRICE RANGE: $$$
NEIGHBORHOOD: Soho
So popular, you need to make reservations far in advance, so plan ahead. The women in the kitchen are not trained chefs in this family owned eatery, but know their stuff just as well as anybody who went to school (better, even). No such thing as a bad dish

from the items on the single page menu offering excellent Indian "home cooking." Favorites: Spiced mutton kabobs; Murgh ka Saalan (boneless chicken thighs) and Goat Kosha Mangsho (slow cooked Bengali goat curry).

DEAN STREET TOWNHOUSE
69 - 71 Dean St, London, +44 207 434 1775
www.deanstreettownhouse.com
CUISINE: British cuisine
DRINKS: Full Bar
SERVING: Breakfast, Lunch, Dinner, Afternoon Tea
PRICE RANGE: $$$
NEIGHBORHOOD: Soho
Located in Soho, this hotel features an all-day dining room with an incredibly long bar and the feel of a private-members-club dining room. The menu features typically British seasonal fare. Menu favorites include: Twice Baked Smoked Haddock Soufflé and Braised Veal Cheeks. Check out the hotel's diverse art collection while you're there with over 60 works of art by artists like Paul Noble, Keith Tyson, Peter Blake, Tracey Emin and Keith Coventry.

THE DELAUNAY

55 Aldwych, London, +44 20 7499 8558

www.thedelaunay.com

CUISINE: British cuisine / Modern European

DRINKS: Full Bar

SERVING: Breakfast, Lunch, Dinner, Afternoon Tea

PRICE RANGE: $$$$

NEIGHBORHOOD: Convent Garden

Inspired by the grand old European cafes, this eatery provides a great dining experience and a décor featuring green leather banquettes, antique mirrors and a marble floor. Menu favorites include: Chicken Curry (often a dish of the day) and Smoke Salmon. You must try the house-baked Austrian cakes. Nice wine list.

DINNER BY HESTON BLUMENTHAL

66 Knightsbridge, London, +44 20 7201 3833
www.dinnerbyheston.com
CUISINE: British cuisine
DRINKS: Full Bar
SERVING: Lunch, Dinner
PRICE RANGE: $$$$
NEIGHBORHOOD: Hyde Park

Located in the **Mandarin Oriental**, this place offers a truly unique dining experience. The menu features historical dishes (pulled from old British cookbooks) like meat fruit (Mandarin, chicken liver & foie gras parfait, grilled bread). Other menu favorites include: Chicken oysters and Grilled octopus. Excellent food, creative cocktails and nice wine pairings. Interesting desserts with choices like the Tipsy Cake - a segmented brioche soaked with icing glaze and served with spit roasted pineapple. Reservations recommended.

THE DRAPERS ARMS

44 Barnsbury St, London, +44 20 7619 0348
www.thedrapersarms.com
CUISINE: British cuisine
DRINKS: Full Bar
SERVING: Lunch & Dinner
PRICE RANGE: $$
NEIGHBORHOOD: Islington
Popular gastropub with a pub feel featuring high ceilings, chandeliers and checkerboard floor. Check out their special events like the American Style BBQ held on July 4th (they even added a few American beers for the day). Favorites: Leg of Lamb. Menu has something for everyone including vegetarian selections. There's a nice garden during good weather.

THE DUKE

7 Roger St, London, 020 7242 7230
www.dukepub.co.uk
CUISINE: Pub Fare
DRINKS: Full Bar
SERVING: Lunch & Dinner; closed Sundays
PRICE RANGE: $$
NEIGHBORHOOD: Bloomsbury
Quiet pub with Art Deco décor featuring a nice menu of authentic British fare. Charles Dickens lived just a few feet away around the corner. Favorites: Cod Filet and Duke's Homemade Burger. Menu changes weekly except for a few favorites like fish and chips.

E. PELLICI

332 Bethnal Green Rd, London, +44 20 7739 4873
www.epellicci.co.uk
CUISINE: Italian
DRINKS: No Booze
SERVING: Breakfast, Lunch
PRICE RANGE: $
NEIGHBORHOOD: Bethnal Green
Popular with locals, this place is a great stop for
breakfast. The Full English breakfast includes grilled
stem mushrooms, grilled tomato halves, sausage,
bacon, and a thick slice of toast with an egg over
easy.

EDWINS

Upstairs 202-206 Borough High St, London, +44 20
7403 9913
www.edwinsborough.co.uk
CUISINE: Bistro
DRINKS: Full Bar
SERVING: Lunch & Dinner; Lunch only on
Saturdays
PRICE RANGE: $$$
NEIGHBORHOOD: Borough
Upstairs eatery looks like a set designer was told to
create the perfect English pub: Tudor-style windows,
large wooden tables, drapes covering the windows—
it's all here. They offer a Modern European menu.
Favorites: Rabbit with spinach polenta and Wood
pigeon with Jerusalem artichoke.

FRYER'S DELIGHT

19 Theobalds Rd, London, +44 20 7405 4114
No Website
CUISINE: Fish & Chips
DRINKS: No Booze
SERVING: Lunch, Dinner
PRICE RANGE: $
NEIGHBORHOOD: Bloomsbury
This cozy little locals' favorite serves up a no-frills
menu. Menu favorites include Cod flakes and
Rockfish. Great bread slattered in butter.

GAME BIRD
The Stafford
16-18 St James's Place, London, +44 20 7493 0111
www.thestaffordlondon.com
CUISINE: British
DRINKS: Full Bar
SERVING: Lunch & Dinner
PRICE RANGE: $$$$
NEIGHBORHOOD: St James's, Green Park
Located in the swellegant Stafford Hotel, this upscale
eatery offers a thoroughgoing tour of solid British
fare. I used to nip in here when I visited my
shirtmaker whose store was just around the corner.
(In fact, it still is.) Never disappointed. It's a bit on
the posh side, traditional, old-school, but thoroughly
charming and soothing. If you've ever wondered what
one of those "gentlemen's clubs" is like, come into

the American Bar (with its tons of memorabilia hanging from the ceiling) and peek into the Game Bird to find out. That's what this place feels like. Favorites: Venison Wellington and Chicken & Duck liver parfait. Vegetarian friendly. Impressive wine list.

GLORIA
54-56 Great Eastern St, London, +44 7903 540051
www.bigmammagroup.com
CUISINE: Italian
DRINKS: Full Bar
SERVING: Breakfast, Lunch, & Dinner 7 days
PRICE RANGE: $$$
NEIGHBORHOOD: Liverpool Street / Broadgate
Upscale and yet extremely comfortable eatery offering Italian classics. The interior is over-decorated on purpose, filled to the point of bursting with knick-knacks, kitschy stuff, decorative plates

lining the walls, plants hanging from the walls, peach-colored upholstery, comfy-loungy seating that feels more like sofas than banquettes. All designed to make you feel at home. Favorites: Carbonara (with the pasta tossed in a hollowed-out wheel of Pecorino); and Truffle pasta. Nice tiramisu. Note that it's open for breakfast, so brunch here on weekends is a sure bet.

THE GREENHOUSE
27-A Hay's Mews, 020-7499-3331
https://www.greenhouserestaurant.co.uk
CUISINE: French - Haute
DRINKS: Full Bar
SERVING: Lunch, Dinner
PRICE RANGE: $$$$
NEIGHBORHOOD: Mayfair
This luxurious eatery serves traditional French cuisine. The place is exceptional in every way, and

fully justifies its 2 Michelin stars, which puts it on a par with the very best spots in London. When the weather is nice, there's nothing finer than to make your way down the garden path that leads to the dining room. The stone artwork you see in the garden is by British sculptor Emily Young. Each dish—and I mean each and every one—is so artfully and meticulously prepared that you'll wonder if you should destroy the masterpiece by eating the damn thing. Trust me, you'll eat it. My Menu picks: Caviar with Cornish Crab and succulent Veal Sweetbreads (from Limousin) served with tasty puffed buckwheat. Exceptional wine list with over 3,400 labels. Reservations recommended.

GYMKHANA
42 Albemarle St, London, +44 20 3011 5900
www.gymkhanalondon.com
CUISINE: Indian
DRINKS: Full Bar
SERVING: Lunch & Dinner; closed Sundays
PRICE RANGE: $$$
NEIGHBORHOOD: Mayfair
The look here is reminiscent of an Englishmen's sporting club set in the British Raj. Popular eatery with tasting menu. Lots of Indian favorites like Chicken Butter Masala or suckling pig vindaloo. If you're not familiar with Indian cuisine you may have to ask for explanations but the staff is friendly and the food is good.

HAKKASAN
8 Hanway Place, London, +44 20 7927 7000
www.hakkasan.com
CUISINE: Chinese
DRINKS: Full Bar
SERVING: Lunch, Dinner
PRICE RANGE: $$
NEIGHBORHOOD: Fitzrovia
Founded in London in 2001, this is the original restaurant of the Hakkasan brand that has now spread all over the world. Here you'll find a new twist on the Chinese fine-dining experience. The dark English oak decorated restaurant features an open kitchen. Menu favorites include: Peking duck with caviar and Grilled Wagyu beef with king soy sauce. Also available is a dim sum menu. Award-winning wine list and menu of signature cocktails.

THE HAVELOCK TAVERN
57 Masbro Rd, London, +44 20 7603 5374

www.havelocktavern.com
CUISINE: Pizza, Mediterranean
DRINKS: Beer & Wine Only
SERVING: Dinner; closed Mondays
PRICE RANGE: $$
NEIGHBORHOOD: West Kensington
Visit this very reasonably priced gastropub serving an
international menu of delicious dishes including duck,
fish and (really good) steaks if you want to avoid the
really pricey nearby eateries in Notting Hill and
Kensington. Menu changes daily. Good ales, cider
and draft beers.

HAWKSMOOR

157 Commercial St, London, +44 20 7426 4850
www.thehawksmoor.com
CUISINE: Steakhouse
DRINKS: Full Bar
SERVING: Lunch, Dinner
PRICE RANGE: $$$$
NEIGHBORHOOD: Spitalfields
This is definitely the place if you're a steak lover.
This steakhouse serves dictionary-thick Longhorn
steaks, the oldest purebred cattle in the U.K. Other
menu favorites include: Grilled Free Range Chicken
and Native Grilled Lobster. For dessert there's a
selection of puddings and, of course, after dinner
drinks.

HÉLÈNE DARROZE AT THE CONNAUGHT

Carlos Place, Mayfair, 020-3147-7200;
www.the-connaught.co.uk/restaurants-bars/helene-darroze-at-the-connaught
CUISINE: French - Haute
DRINKS: Full Bar
SERVING: Lunch, Dinner
PRICE RANGE: $$$$
NEIGHBORHOOD: Mayfair

This is one of Mayfair's most elegant and posh Michelin dining experiences, with its blond-stained wooden paneling giving the room a more casual feel as you gaze through the windows toward the leafy trees in the square across the street. This eatery serves exquisite upscale French cuisine using the best ingredients money can buy. (They buy the ingredients first, and you buy them second, with a hefty mark-up.) The duck comes from France. The lobster from Cornwall. You get the idea. If you can't get a good meal here, you're *very* hard to please. Comprehensive wine list. Reservations recommended. You can't actually go wrong eating anywhere in the Connaught.

Don't forget that **Jean-Georges** has a big presence here with his eponymous dining room. He not only has his signature named restaurant here, with its floor-to-ceiling windows offering a beautiful view of the square, but he runs the famous **Connaught Grill** as well. I can't stand what they've done with the old Grill. They've stripped it down to the point that it looks like a tarted up version of a Hungry Sizzler steak house in some backwater town in Mississippi. Very sad. It's almost worth just getting a bite at one of the intimate bars here. There's the **Connaught Bar** and the **Coburg Bar,** both of which are very clubby, dark, intimate and nice. They each have small plate menus that will do you very nicely. Like all the great hotels in the world, it's not in the least important where you eat in any of them. It's only important that you experience the wonder of some of these grand pleasure palaces. And you can do that for the price of a cocktail expertly prepared. By the way, there's also a very fine **Afternoon Tea** in the Connaught. You certainly don't want to pass through London without indulging in Afternoon Tea. The English do it better than anybody else.

HEREFORD ROAD

3 Hereford Rd, Westbourne Grove, London, +44 20 7727 1144

www.herefordroad.org

CUISINE: British cuisine

DRINKS: Full Bar

SERVING: Lunch, Dinner

PRICE RANGE: $$$$

NEIGHBORHOOD: Notting Hill

Just above the Bayswater Road is this elegant restaurant with an excellent menu of fresh English cuisine. Chef Tom Pemberton takes food preparation seriously and customers get to see most of the work in the open kitchen. Menu favorites include: Deviled duck livers and Lamb Rump with purple sprouting broccoli; roasted quail with aioli; braised cuttlefish; cold roasted duck breast with pickled chicory, artichokes and roasted shallots; whole braised lamb's neck (I know it sounds awful, but it's delicious). A no-frills but delightful experience.

HIDE ABOVE
85 Piccadilly, Mayfair, 020-3146-8666
http://hide.co.uk
CUISINE: European (Modern)
DRINKS: Full Bar
SERVING: Breakfast, Lunch, Dinner
PRICE RANGE: $$$$
NEIGHBORHOOD: Mayfair
This is a modern three-level restaurant offering a fun
and elegant dining experience. Very sleek, very
modern, very industrial, dramatic lighting, a bustling
crowd, lots of fun. You forget how stiff and stuffy
those other Michelin-starred restaurants can be when
you pop into a place like this throwing off an electric
vibe, thrumming with excitement and vitality. High

above Piccadilly, you can get a good view of Green Park. This place is just as good for any meal, breakfast, lunch or dinner. Menu picks: Roasted Scallops and Roasted Herdwick Lamb with Smoked Cockles. I'd never had a smoked cockle before, but I did here. Incredible wine selection and the prices aren't as devastating as a lot of other places working at this level of sophistication. The entire place seems to be made of wood. Late night dining. Lunch is a la carte, dinner is tasting menus only. Reservations recommended.

HIX SOHO
66-70 Brewer St, London, +44 20 7292 3518
www.hixsoho.co.uk
CUISINE: British cuisine
DRINKS: Full Bar
SERVING: Lunch & Dinner
PRICE RANGE: $$$
NEIGHBORHOOD: Soho
Restaurant serving primarily British cuisine. Favorites: Hanger steak and Chopped short rib burger. Great cocktails – downstairs is the cocktail bar with an atmosphere all its own.

IKOYI

1 St James's Market, London, +44 20 3583 4660
www.ikoyilondon.com
CUISINE: African (West Africa)
DRINKS: Full Bar
SERVING: Lunch & Dinner
PRICE RANGE: $$$
NEIGHBORHOOD: St James's
Chic eatery with an African décor serving authentic West African cuisine. (It's good enough to have a Michelin star.) It's in odd contrast to the highly traditional St. James's area, but that's what makes it fun. Ultra-modern décor. They have a 7-course tasting menu that changes frequently, and you'll be surprised how fresh and different this food is. Dishes are meticulously plated. Favorites: Crab meat custard; Honey Butter Pumpkin. Creative cocktails.

THE IVY

1-5 West St, London +44 20 7836 4751
www.the-ivy.co.uk/

CUISINE: Modern European
DRINKS: Full Bar
SERVING: Lunch, Dinner
PRICE RANGE: $$$
NEIGHBORHOOD: Covent Garden
This old school restaurant offers a simple menu of really good food. This well-known eatery is a favorite of celebrities and politicians-even at lunch. Menu favorites include: Bang-bang chicken and Herb-roasted salmon. Dessert selection includes Crème Brule and Chocolate Fondant. Impressive wine list. Upstairs there's a private members' club. Reservations recommended.

JOSE
104 Bermondsey St, London, +44 20 7403 4902
www.josepizarro.com
CUISINE: Spanish, Tapas Bars
DRINKS: Beer & Wine Only
SERVING: Lunch, Dinner
PRICE RANGE: $$
NEIGHBORHOOD: Borough
This is a standing room-only in this very bustling joint that serves authentic Spanish tapas like prawns *a la plancha*. Menu favorites include: tomato bread, pimentos de Padron, chorizo, Iberico pork cheek, hake, and mixed cheeses. Nice wine offerings. Menu changes daily.

KILN
58 Brewer St, London, **No Phone**
www.kilnsoho.com
CUISINE: Thai
DRINKS: Full Bar
SERVING: Lunch & Dinner; Closed Saturdays
PRICE RANGE: $$
NEIGHBORHOOD: Soho
Casual eatery with an open kitchen serving noodles &
Thai-inspired dishes (a lot of them very spicy, wow!).
Try to sit at the counter, even if it involves a wait.
Much more exciting experience. Favorites: Aged
Lamb & Cumin Skewer; Fried monkfish; Clay Pot
Baked Glass Noodles. No reservations unless you're
in a group.

KITTY FISHER'S WOOD GRILL

10 Shepherd Market, London, +44 20 3302 1661
www.kittyfishers.com
CUISINE: British cuisine
DRINKS: Full Bar
SERVING: Lunch & Dinner; Dinner only on
Saturdays; closed Sundays
PRICE RANGE: $$$$
NEIGHBORHOOD: Mayfair
Dimly lit small eatery in historic Shepherd Market
that seats about 40 people in an elegant setting that
will leave no doubt you're in Mayfair, with its gold-
framed art pieces, red banquettes, elaborate sconces.
Menu is modern British fare with a Spanish twist.
Favorites: Cornish crab with BBQ'd cucumber and
Whipped cod roe on bread. Good cocktail and wine
menu.

KRICKET

12 Denman St, Soho, London, +44 20 7734 5612
www.kricket.co.uk
CUISINE: Indian / Anglo-Indian
DRINKS: Full Bar (with great specialty cocktails)
SERVING: Lunch & Dinner; Closed Sundays
PRICE RANGE: $$
NEIGHBORHOOD: Soho
Funky joint serving Indian-inspired small plates. On
the first floor they welcome walk-in traffic, while
below in the basement there is service at communal
tables with reservations. The only problem with that
is it's more exciting upstairs at the bar. I advise going
a little earlier and taking your chance for a seat or
wait for one. Favorites: Tandoori grouse; Keralan
fried chicken (very flavorful & spicy); and Coorgi
Pork Cheek. Reservations recommended.

LA BODEGA NEGRA

16 Moor St, London, +44 20 7758 4100

www.labodeganegra.com
CUISINE: Mexican
DRINKS: Full Bar
SERVING: Lunch, Dinner
PRICE RANGE: $$$
NEIGHBORHOOD: Bloomsbury
Guests enter through a faux sex shop front similar to an old speakeasy of the 1930s. The place definitely has a buzz and you feel like you've just entered a party. Of course the margaritas are plentiful and the menu is typical Mexican fare. Menu favorites include: Seafood cazuela (similar to paella) and Lamb shank. The experience may surpass the cuisine but it's definitely a fun visit.

LA FAMIGLIA

7 Langton St, The World's End, London, +44 20 7351 0761
www.lafamiglia.co.uk
CUISINE: Italian, Gluten-Free
DRINKS: Beer & Wine
SERVING: Lunch, Dinner
PRICE RANGE: $$$
NEIGHBORHOOD: Chelsea
This well-known eatery serves authentic Italian cuisine. Menu favorites include: Lobster pasta and Fried battered mozzarella. Delicious bread and bread sticks. Also a great place for Sunday brunch. Reservations recommended.

LA GAVROCHE

43 Upper Brook St, London, +44 20 7408 0881
www.le-gavroche.co.uk
CUISINE: French
DRINKS: Full Bar
SERVING: Lunch, Dinner
PRICE RANGE: $$$$
NEIGHBORHOOD: Marylebone
This fine-dining establishment offers top-notch
classical French cuisine from Michel Roux, Jr. Here
you'll find their justifiably famous cheese soufflé
along with hot foie gras on a crisp duck pancake with
cinnamon. Menu favorites include the Loin of
Venison with walnut gnocchi. Desserts include
apricot and Cointreau soufflés, which will melt in
your mouth. The wine list is excellent with a selection
of top French wines.

THE LEDBURY

127 Ledbury Rd, London, +44 20 7792 9090
www.theledbury.com

CUISINE: Modern European
DRINKS: Full Bar
SERVING: Lunch, Dinner
PRICE RANGE: $$$$
NEIGHBORHOOD: Notting Hill
This trendy spot offers a savory menu with delights such as Loin and Shoulder of lamb and Roast Sea Bass. Desserts are just as tasty with choices like: Passion Fruit Soufflé with Sauternes Ice Cream and Banana and Chocolate Malt Tartlet. If you can book a table it's definitely a pleasing experience.

LE MANOIR AUX QUAF'SAISONS
Church Rd, Great Milton, Oxford, +44 1844 278881
www.manoir.com
CUISINE: French
DRINKS: Full Bar
SERVING: Lunch, Dinner
PRICE RANGE: $$$$
NEIGHBORHOOD: London Bridge
A favorite of foodies, this eatery is for those with a passion for food. The chefs use the freshest and best quality ingredients, most from their two-acre garden. Try the 6-course tasting menu for a nice variety. Menu favorites include the Summer Vegetable Risotto. Their wine cellar boasts approximately 1,000

different wines from around the world. An experience you won't forget. Reservations necessary.

LOCANDA LOCATELLI
8 Seymour St, Marylebone, 020-7935 8390

www.locandalocatelli.com
CUISINE: Italian
DRINKS: Full Bar
SERVING: Lunch, Dinner
PRICE RANGE: $$$$
NEIGHBORHOOD: Marylebone
Elegant eatery serving classic Italian fare with a twist in a nice location next to the Churchill Hotel in an elegant room with modern decor. A very lively crowd comes to this Michelin-starred place, which is without question one of the best Italian restaurants in all London. Favorites: Linguine with Cornish Lobster and Sliced cured pork belly. Extensive wine list. Reservations recommended.

LYLE'S
Tea Building
56 Shoreditch High St, London, +44 20 3011 5911
www.lyleslondon.com
CUISINE: British
DRINKS: Full Bar
SERVING: Breakfast, Lunch & Dinner; closed Sundays
PRICE RANGE: $$$
NEIGHBORHOOD: Shoreditch
Simple industrial-style eatery offering a menu of seasonal British fare. The set menu changes daily, depending on what the chef wants to cook, and his decision is made based on what he's able to get from his specially selected suppliers. The chef says, "I think of it as commonsense cooking, buying from good fishermen, good farms, from people of similar mindset, just sensible, not reinventing the wheel."

Warning: don't stuff yourself with the plentiful delicious sourdough bread. Twice I've ruined my dinner gobbling down too much of this delicious bread. Favorites: Lamb Sweetbreads and Mutton tartare. Try the Caramel Ice Cream for dessert. The wine list here is nicely affordable.

MEATLIQUOR
74 Welbeck St, London, +44 20 7224 4239
www.meatliquor.com
CUISINE: Burgers
DRINKS: Full Bar
SERVING: Lunch, Dinner
PRICE RANGE: $$
NEIGHBORHOOD: Marylebone
Meatliquor offers a club-like atmosphere starting at the door where you're greeted by two doormen. Inside, the feel is more like a dark and loud nightclub than restaurant and note signs announce "no suits" and "no ballet pumps". This place is known for its burgers and they come in varieties like: Dead Hippie Burger and Buffalo Chicken Burger. They also serve great cheese fries. Party atmosphere so it's a perfect place for a fun birthday. Go early to avoid the wait.

MILK
18-20 Bedford Hill, London, +44 4420 8772 9085
www.milk.london
CUISINE: British
DRINKS: Full Bar
SERVING: Breakfast, Lunch & Dinner; closed Sundays
PRICE RANGE: $$$

NEIGHBORHOOD: Balham
Popular local café known for its specialty coffees and innovative cuisine. The atmosphere is very cozy, homey, like an old farmhouse, with simple wooden tables, old wallpaper. Everything is made from scratch, so you'll love it as much as I did. Favorites: Crumpets with goat's curd and honey and "Young Betty" (poached eggs with bacon and hollandaise on sourdough). Outdoor seating.

MONOCLE CAFÉ
18 Chiltern St, London, +44 20 7135 2040
www.monocle.com/about/contacts/london-cafe
CUISINE: Coffee & Tea
DRINKS: Beer & Wine
SERVING: Sweets & Baked goods
PRICE RANGE: $$
NEIGHBORHOOD: Marylebone
Great place for coffee and sweets like pastries and baked goods from Stockholm's Fabrique bakery.

Other offerings include: Japanese chocolate bars and rollcake.

NEPTUNE
Principal Hotel
Corner Guilford St & Russell Sq, London, +44 20 7123 5000
www.neptune.london
CUISINE: Seafood
DRINKS: Full Bar
SERVING: Lunch & Dinner Mon – Fri; Dinner only Sat & Sun
PRICE RANGE: $$$$
NEIGHBORHOOD: Bloomsbury
Modern seafood-focused eatery with an oyster bar. Extensive menu. Favorites: White Lobster, Wild mussels with saffron, bay leaf and orange sofritto; Rump steak. Elegant dining. Wine list mostly French.

Ottolenghi

OTTOLENGHI

287 Upper St, London, +44 20 7288 1454
www.ottolenghi.co.uk
CUISINE: Mediterranean
DRINKS: Beer & Wine Only
SERVING: Breakfast, Lunch, & Dinner
PRICE RANGE: $$
NEIGHBORHOOD: Islington

Both a restaurant and a deli, this happening place is designed so that it looks and feels like a retail store that ought to be selling high fashion. Instead, it's a restaurant with salads on the counter that change daily. Try to come in the evening when they bring out the candles and the place becomes more sophisticated. Weekend brunch is too crowded, so come during a weekday. Don't overlook the delectable jarred items you can buy in the deli. Favorites: Roasted Aubergine (eggplant) and Burrata with butternut squash. Breakfast—get the Dutch baby pancake with poached fruit. Communal dining. Reservations for dinner only. Popular pre-theatre destination.

Ottolenghi

PADELLA
6 Southwark St, London, **no phone**
www.padella.co
CUISINE: Italian
DRINKS: Beer & Wine Only
SERVING: Lunch & Dinner; no reservations
PRICE RANGE: $$
NEIGHBORHOOD: London Bridge
Modern bistro with a small menu of Italian cuisine.
This place is lots of fun. If you go for lunch, you'll
have to wait in a line, but if you go for dinner, you
put your name in and they will text you when the
table's ready. Meantime, you go to one of the many
nearby pubs in Borough-Market and have a drink.
Opt for the upstairs, which is busier at the counters
where you can watch the cooks hand-rolling pasta.
Downstairs is a more intimate, so decide on your
mood. For the quality of the pasta here, the prices are

very affordable. So a lot of locals frequent the place. (To be honest, the portions are a little on the small side, so order a third dish—it's cheap enough.) Favorites: Pappardelle with the beef-shin ragu (their specialty); and Gnocchi with nutmeg butter. Nice wine list. No reservations, you need to show up 30-45 minutes before the restaurant opens at 5 p.m. Very busy. You can add your name to the queue on their website.

PALOMAR
34 Rupert St, London, +44 20 7439 8777
www.thepalomar.co.uk
CUISINE: Middle Eastern/Mediterranean
DRINKS: Full Bar
SERVING: Lunch & Dinner
PRICE RANGE: $$$
NEIGHBORHOOD: Soho
Unique eatery offering Modern fare from Jerusalem with an international twist. The kubaneh and tzatziki were amazing. But here it's really about the excitement level created by a smart staff and hip diners. Favorites: Octo-hummous and Beetroot carpaccio. Open kitchen so you can watch the food being prepared.

PIDGIN
52 Wilton Way, London, +44 20 7254 8311
www.pidginlondon.com
CUISINE: British (but Asian inspired)
DRINKS: Full Bar
SERVING: Dinner, Lunch & Dinner on Sat & Sun
PRICE RANGE: $$$

NEIGHBORHOOD: Hackney
Small simple eatery offering Asian-inspired/European cuisine that's impossible to categorize. They serve the same 4-course set menu for lunch and dinner, with the menu changing every week. (The pride themselves on not repeating a dish for over a year.) Example of a recent menu at press time: Haddock with wonton; sourdough, brown butter; Scallop, clam, land cress & black currant; Pork with sweet potato & oregano; Duck, grelot, cocoa nib; a couple of interesting desserts. Whatever they concoct, you'll love it. Trust me. Never been disappointed here, ever. Quite romantic at night. Nice wine list.

PIZARRO
194 Bermondsey St, London, +44 20 7378 9455
www.josepizarro.com/pizarro-restaurant/
WEBSITE DOWN AT PRESSTIME
CUISINE: Spanish
DRINKS: Full Bar
SERVING: Lunch & Dinner
PRICE RANGE: $$
NEIGHBORHOOD: Borough
Large modern restaurant fitted out like a warehouse, with its brick walls, large planked floors, old chandeliers and fixtures. They serve tapas and contemporary Spanish fare. Set menu with a variety of starters. Favorites: sweetbreads with mustard and mayo and girolle mushrooms with Manchego & truffle oil.

POLLEN STREET SOCIAL

8/10 Pollen St, London, +44 20 7290 7600
www.pollenstreetsocial.com
CUISINE: British
DRINKS: Full Bar
SERVING: Lunch, Dinner
PRICE RANGE: $$$$
NEIGHBORHOOD: Marylebone

Chef Jason Atherton of Ramsay's Maze offers a
casual dining menu that includes eight starters and
eight mains. Menu favorites include: Roasted Atlantic
Halibut and Lake District rack of lamb. Vegetarian
selections available. Desserts feature the signature
"PBJ" – a peanut parfait and Goat's milk rice pudding
with goat's cheese ice-cream. The wine list is quite
large and there's also a nice selection of lagers.

QUO VADIS

26-29 Dean St, London, +44 20 7437 9585
www.quovadissoho.co.uk
CUISINE: Seafood
DRINKS: Full Bar
SERVING: Lunch, Dinner
PRICE RANGE: $$$
NEIGHBORHOOD: Soho
Open since 1926, this charming little restaurant serves
primarily modern British cuisine. Menu changes
daily. Menu favorites include: Shepherd's Pie and
Breast of Lamb. Pre-theatre menu for the theatre
crowd. Nice cocktails. Private club upstairs.

RABOT 1745

2-4 Bedale St, London, +44 20 7378 8226
www.hotelchocolat.com
CUISINE: American (New)
DRINKS: Full Bar

SERVING: Breakfast, Lunch & Dinner
PRICE RANGE: $$
NEIGHBORHOOD: Borough Market
Ideal choice for chocolate lovers. A slightly
pretentious chocolate shop/restaurant/Café offering a
variety of chocolate choices from hot chocolate to
spiced chocolate. Almost all the food has a form of
chocolate as an ingredient, like the carpaccio Rabot,
topped with cacao-liquor dressing. Great take-away
service as well.

RANDALL & AUBIN
14- 16 Brewer St, London, +44 20 7287 4447
www.randallandaubin.com
CUISINE: Seafood/British
DRINKS: Full Bar
SERVING: Lunch, Dinner
PRICE RANGE: $$$
NEIGHBORHOOD: Soho
This hip eatery is a great choice for a date or hanging
with friends. Here you'll find an excellent choice of
seafood and French and English dishes. Nice wine
list. Menu favorites include: Seafood platter (enough
for two) and Rotisserie chicken. Extensive wine list.

RESTAURANT STORY
199 Tooley St, London, +44 20 7183 2117
www.restaurantstory.co.uk
CUISINE: Pizza, Mediterranean
DRINKS: Beer & Wine Only
SERVING: Lunch & Dinner; closed Sunday &
Monday
PRICE RANGE: $$$$

NEIGHBORHOOD: London Bridge; Bermondsey
Just on the south bank of the Thames in a high-ceilinged room with floor to ceiling glass windows that give it an open, airy feel is this this Michelin-starred eatery where you can choose between two menus – 6 or 10 courses. All courses come with delicious warm homemade bread. Favorites: Scallops, cucumber and dill ash and Beef tartare, apple and Perigord truffle. Truly an unforgettable dining experience.

THE RIDING HOUSE CAFÉ
43-51 Great Titchfield St, London, +44 20 7927 0840
www.ridinghousecafe.co.uk
CUISINE: British/Tapas
DRINKS: Full Bar
SERVING: Brunch, Lunch, Dinner
PRICE RANGE: $$
NEIGHBORHOOD: Fitzrovia
This hipster chic brasserie attracts a variety of crowds depending on the time of day you may be seated next to film execs or media brass. Dinner menu favorites include: Lobster lasagna and Venison Haunch. Known for their signature cocktails and impressive wine list. Dessert choices include: Baked Alaska and Sticky Toffee Pudding.

Restaurant Terrace, The Ritz

THE RITZ RESTAURANT

150 Piccadilly, 020-7300 2370
www.theritzlondon.com/dine-with-us/the-ritz-restaurant
CUISINE: European (Modern) / British
DRINKS: Full Bar
SERVING: Breakfast, Lunch, Dinner
PRICE RANGE: $$$$
NEIGHBORHOOD: St James's

Visiting the Ritz is like going to Buckingham Palace or the British Museum. It's a quintessential English thing to do. I could say the same thing about Claridge's or Brown's hotel or any number of other places, but the Ritz always stands out. The elegant marble columns and sumptuous décor of its public rooms, the fine quality of its restaurant and bar offerings—it's all very hard to beat. If the weather's good, try hard to get a table out on the **Restaurant Terrace at the Ritz**. The lovely flower boxes are bursting with color and you'll get a view of Green Park from up here. There's another little gem called the **Secret Garden Bar**, but the Terrace is more memorable. You'll never forget those flower boxes. The main dining room at the Ritz is not fun. It's gorgeous, don't get me wrong. Just so stuffy and formal. You'll feel like you're dining in an aristocrat's house, but that he doesn't really want you there as a guest. Take a peek in just to see what it looks like, but eat in one of the other rooms. Overall, this is an upscale eatery in a baroque setting serving British/French cuisine. Menu picks: Loin of Venison with smoked parsnip and the classic Beef Wellington. (I love parsnips, but a lot of people don't.) There's **Afternoon Tea**, of course, one of the best in town. And don't overlook the charming intimate dark bars here at the Ritz. It's not the Paris Ritz, but it's close enough.

Main dining room, The Ritz

ROGANIC
5-7 Blandford St, Marylebone, 020-3370-6260
www.roganic.uk
CUISINE: British (Modern)
DRINKS: Full Bar
SERVING: Lunch, Dinner
PRICE RANGE: $$$$
NEIGHBORHOOD: Marylebone
Upscale dining with a menu of modern British
cuisine. The chef here is Simon Rogan. He had a
place up in the Lake District, and some of the produce
you get here will come from his farm up there. It's all
about high quality cuisine from some of the finest
purveyors in the country served in a casual, low-
pressure atmosphere. Sleek modern décor and a lively
fun crowd. Favorites: Beef tendon with pike perch
and Native Oyster with trout roe. There's a tasting

menu or you can go a la carte. Impressive wine list. Reservations recommended. The same people own **AULIS**, a tiny little place in Soho where they experiment with dishes some of which might later be served here.

ROCHELLE CANTEEN AT THE ICA
Rochelle School
16 Playground Gardens , London, +44 20 7729 5677
https://www.ica.art/rochelle-canteen
CUISINE: European / Café
DRINKS: Limited cocktail selection
SERVING: Breakfast & Lunch daily, Dinner on Fridays & Saturdays
PRICE RANGE: $$
NEIGHBORHOOD: Shoreditch, Bethnal Green
Hidden behind a green door, access offers outdoor dining in a courtyard. This is right off The Mall at the foot of Carlton House Terrace. A very simple place, there's a sake bar on the ground floor and a white-walled restaurant up on the mezzanine. Menu changes daily, so you never know, but it's always something good. More casual snacks at the sake bar, which is always busy with an artsy young crowd. Upstairs at night they'll put candles on the tables, but it's still very basic. Favorites: Rillettes with pickled cucumber; Spring morels with baked eggs and Grilled squid with chick peas. BYOB. Reservations recommended.

SALON
18 Market Row, London, +44 20 7501 9152
www.salonbrixton.co.uk

CUISINE: British
DRINKS: Full Bar
SERVING: Dinner, Lunch on Sat & Sun; closed on Mondays
PRICE RANGE: $$$
NEIGHBORHOOD: Coldharbour Lane/ Herne Hill / Brixton
Downstairs is the deli and upstairs it the restaurant – using ingredients from the deli. Great tasting menu of traditional British fare. Nice wine list. Reservations recommended.

SCOTT'S
20 Mount St, London, +44 20 7495 7309
www.scotts-restaurant.com
CUISINE: Seafood, British
DRINKS: Full Bar

SERVING: Lunch, Dinner
PRICE RANGE: $$$$
NEIGHBORHOOD: Mayfair
This is one of London's great fish restaurants from the people who own the Ivy and Le Caprice. Here you'll find great seafood and a grand oyster bar as the restaurant's centerpiece. Menu favorites include: Bass ceviche and Halibut Fillet. Check out the champagne and oyster bar. Here you'll find an impressive cocktail menu and wine list that complements the varied menu. Save room for the delicious desserts like the Bakewell pudding.

SEXY FISH
@ BERKELEY SQUARE HOUSE
4-6 Berkeley Sq, London, +44 20 3764 2000
www.sexyfish.com
CUISINE: Japanese/Asian Fusion
DRINKS: Full Bar
SERVING: Lunch & Dinner

PRICE RANGE: $$$$
NEIGHBORHOOD: Mayfair
Upscale, art-filled eatery focusing primarily on Asian fish and shellfish. Worth coming here for the wonderful design—there are floating fish lamps designed by Frank Gehry, hand cut collage art adorning the ceiling designed by Michael Roberts, bronze mermaids cast by Damien Hirst, unusual lightning fixtures. The bar here is spectacular. Favorites: Miso Chilean sea bass and Yellowtail with smoked tofu and caviar. Creative desserts like warm out of the over cinnamon donuts.

SOIF
27 Battersea Rise, London, +44 20 7223 1112
www.soif.co
CUISINE: British
DRINKS: Full Bar
SERVING: Breakfast, Lunch & Dinner; closed Sundays
PRICE RANGE: $$$
NEIGHBORHOOD: Clapham Common, Clapham Junction
Cute little eatery serving up a combination of British and French fare – mostly small plates. Menu picks: Beef tartare and Quail with harissa and yogurt. Impressive wine list – mostly French labels.

SMOKEHOUSE
63-69 Canonbury Rd, London, +44 20 7354 1144
www.smokehouseislington.co.uk
CUISINE: Smokehouse
DRINKS: Full Bar

SERVING: Dinner, Lunch on Sat & Sun
PRICE RANGE: $$$
NEIGHBORHOOD: Canonbury, Islington
Upscale smokehouse offering a small a-la carte menu of smoked and grilled food. Favorites: Short-rib bourguignon and any of the steaks. 20 craft beers on tap and 40 in a bottle. Wine list of small family producers only.

SPRING
Somerset House
New Wing Lancaster Place, London, + 44 20 3011 0115
www.springrestaurant.co.uk
CUISINE: Modern European / British
DRINKS: Lunch, Dinner, & Brunch
SERVING: Lunch & Dinner
PRICE RANGE: $$$$

NEIGHBORHOOD: Strand
Located inside the new wing of the Somerset House, this upscale eatery offers a creative menu of European fare. The atmosphere is cool, calm, collected. Lots of white is used in the décor, giving the place a bright, cherry feeling, but also a lot of formality. The peach-colored chairs offer a little break from the cool white interior. (I think they're peach—I am a little bit color-blind in that shade.) At night the place is transformed into an utterly elegant, romantic room, with soft lighting that even flattered me. Favorites: Wild halibut with roasted endive and Filet of beef. Curated wine list.

ST JOHN
26 St John St, London, +44 20 7251 0848
www.stjohngroup.uk.com
CUISINE: British
DRINKS: Full Bar
SERVING: Lunch, Dinner
PRICE RANGE: $$$
NEIGHBORHOOD: Farringdon
This place is for meat lovers and the mezzanine dining room is located in the former Smithfield smokehouse. Menu favorites include: Bone Marrow and Grouse and Deviled kidneys. Wine list of all French wines.

SWEETINGS FISH RESTAURANT
39 Queen Victoria St, London, +44 20 7248 3062
www.sweetingsrestaurant.co.uk/
CUISINE: British
DRINKS: No Booze

SERVING: Lunch only
PRICE RANGE: $$$
NEIGHBORHOOD: The City
First opened in 1889, this restaurant now offers a wide variety of sustainable fish. Menu favorites include: the classic Fish Pie might be the best of its kind in all London; Smoked Trout is good; the crab and smoked fish rolls will not disappoint. Nice wine list to complement fish dishes. Homemade puddings for dessert.

TERROIRS
5 William IV St, London, +44 20 7036 0660
www.terroirswinebar.com
CUISINE: French
DRINKS: Beer & Wine Only
SERVING: Lunch, Dinner
PRICE RANGE: $$

NEIGHBORHOOD: Covent Garden
This two-level wine bar and restaurant offers a
selection of over 200 French and Italian wines but
specializes in "natural wines." The menu offers a
variety of simple dishes: charcuterie, tapas, and
French-inspired dishes. Menu favorites include:
Blackened Shoulder of Lamb and Cod in Brown
Shrimp Butter. Delicious dessert choices include:
Bitter Chocolate Pot Pudding and Yorkshire Rhubarb
Pudding.

TRAMSHED
32 Rivington St, London, +44 20 7749 0478
www.chickenandsteak.co.uk
CUISINE: British, Steakhouse
DRINKS: Full Bar
SERVING: Lunch, Dinner
PRICE RANGE: $$
NEIGHBORHOOD: Hoxton

This artsy restaurant offers a simple menu of steak and chicken. This is meat-lovers' heaven with nice big steaks ideal for sharing and if you're a fan of chicken order the Chicken on the Bone, a whole chicken that comes with fries. Good cocktail and wine selection.

WILTONS
55 Jermyn St, London, +44 20 7629 9955
www.wiltons.co.uk
CUISINE: Seafood
DRINKS: Full Bar
SERVING: Lunch, Dinner
PRICE RANGE: $$$$
NEIGHBORHOOD: Piccadilly

Established in 1742, this iconic restaurant continues serving great traditional English cuisine in an atmosphere that evokes the great private gentlemen's clubs of London. The menu is filled with items like wild fish (the Dover sole is exquisite), shellfish (Queen Victoria awarded them a Royal Warrant as purveyors of oysters to the Crown in 1884) and game in season. Menu favorites include: Fillet of Cod and Sharphan park spelt risotto. Impressive wine list. Delicious desserts include the Morello cherry and chocolate soufflé. Seasonal menu.

THE WOLSELEY
160 Piccadilly, London, +44 20 7499 6996
www.thewolseley.com
CUISINE: Cafe
DRINKS: Full Bar
SERVING: Breakfast, Lunch, Dinner

PRICE RANGE: $$$
NEIGHBORHOOD: Mayfair
If you're one for impeccable service, this high-ceilinged Art Deco gem is the place. Here you'll get white-glove service in the grand European tradition. Known for its wonderful breakfast cuisine (get the very English "kedgeree," an Anglo-Indian inspired dish consisting of curried rice and smoked haddock with a poached egg served on top), the other menus are just as impressive. Menu favorites include: Steak Tartare and Grilled Halibut. Great place for afternoon tea. Reservations recommended.

WRIGHT BROTHERS OYSTER & PORTER HOUSE
11 Stoney St, London, +44 20 7403 9554
www.thewrightbrothers.co.uk/
CUISINE: Seafood
DRINKS: Full Bar
SERVING: Lunch, Dinner
PRICE RANGE: $$$
NEIGHBORHOOD: London Bridge / Borough Market
This restaurant has a fast turnover and all the seating is high-backed stools. Menu changes daily and is written on a blackboard over the bar. If the weather permits, try to secure one of the big wooden barrels outside that serve as tables. Menu favorites include: Oysters Japanese-style and Grilled Plaice. Great place for Sunday brunch with menu choices like: smoked haddock kedgeree, and scrambled eggs with Hederman's organic smoked salmon. Nice wine list.

NIGHTLIFE

214 BERMONDSEY

214 Bermondsey St, London, +44 20 7403 6875
www.two1four.com
NEIGHBORHOOD: Borough
Underneath the **Flour & Grape**, this small
downstairs bar offers a fun drinking experience.
You'd never find this place unless somebody like me
alerted you to it. Brick walls, dim lighting, lots of
candles. If you're not into gin, this place may change

your mind. Great collection of gins but there are alternative cocktails for non-gin drinkers.

BAR ITALIA
22 Frith St, Soho, London, +44 20 7437 4737
www.baritaliasoho.co.uk
NEIGHBORHOOD: Bloomsbury
This is a traditional 24-hour coffee bar where you can get authentic Italian coffee, Portuguese custards, and pannini sandwiches. The barista behind the counter is genuine and so is the coffee. Not a lounging sort of place but a 'get your espresso and go' place. Also don't ask for complicated concoctions that you might order at Starbucks.

BLIND PIG
58 Poland St, London, +44 20 7993 3251
www.socialeatinghouse.com
NEIGHBORHOOD: Soho
Great bar with character – something out of Harry Potter if he was old enough to drink. This speakeasy style spot has a blind with a blindfold on to welcome you. Excellent cocktails served by bartenders who know their stuff. Small creative menu of bar grub. Trendy types, media types, all types who love the downstairs **Social Eating House** bistro located downstairs.

BLIND SPOT
St. Martins Hotel
Covent Garden, 45 St Martin's Ln, London, +44 20 7300 5588
www.morganshotelgroup.com

NEIGHBORHOOD: Covent Garden
Chic and secret cocktail bar located in the luxury St. Martins Hotel designed by Phillipe Starck featuring low lighting and eclectic art. Great cocktails.

BOOKING OFFICE BAR
Euston Road, King's Cross, London, +44 20 7841 3566
www.the-booking-office.com
NEIGHBORHOOD: King's Cross
Located in the St Pancras Renaissance London Hotel, a beautiful bar with incredible architectural features from the original old station. Cocktail menu features variety of punches and mixed drinks from lost recipes from another era.

CADENHEAD'S WHISKEY SHOP & TASTING ROOM

26 Chiltern St, London, +44 20 7935 6999
www.whiskytastingroom.com
NEIGHBORHOOD: Marylebone
This one of a kind whiskey bottler offers spirits from distilleries from all over Scotland and bottles them without filtration. Chalkboards feature an extensive list of rare scotches, which are available for sampling in the tasting room.

CAT & MUTTON

76 Broadway Market, London, +44 20 7249 6555
www.catandmutton.com
NEIGHBORHOOD: Broadway Market, London Fields
Traditional gastropub with a great selection of creative cocktails. Bloody Marys and Bloody Caesars. Check out their Sunday Roasts where they have great

selection of food. Theme nights like Wednesday quiz night. Draws artists and sports fans.

CRAFT LONDON
Peninsula Square, London, +44 20 8465 5910
https://craft-london.co.uk/
NEIGHBORHOOD: Greenwich
Located on the third floor, this hip new British eatery is also a café, cocktail bar and shop. Delicious craft cocktails and imaginative cuisine, like the langoustines with lardo, or the clay-baked duck.

CRAZY COQS
20 Sherwood St, London, +44 20 7734 4888
www.brasseriezedel.com/crazy-coqs
NEIGHBORHOOD: Soho
Jazz & Blues nightclub-cabaret. Intimate room for great performances. Check out the open mike night.

DUCK & WAFFLE
110 Bishopsgate, 40th Floor, London, +44 20 3640 7310
www.duckandwaffle.com
NEIGHBORHOOD: Aldgate
Upscale bar and eatery offering traditional British cuisine. Top-notch cocktails in a beautiful spot that welcomes guests 24/7. Dress code. Reservations necessary.

MARK'S BAR
SOHO - HIX, 66-70 Brewer St, London, +44 20 7292 3518
www.marksbar.co.uk
NEIGHBORHOOD: Soho
The downstairs bar at Mark Hix's venture has already been labeled a hot spot with its leather couches and ambient lighting. This is a comfortable clubby bar that serves creative cocktails with a great little menu of bar snacks. This place gets busy and unless you're having dinner upstairs or know the crew, you may have a difficult time at the door. They even have bar billiards.

OPIUM

15-16 Gerrard St, London, +44 20 7734 7276
www.opiumchinatown.com
NEIGHBORHOOD: Chinatown
This place has the feel of an old speakeasy/opium
den. There's a mixology school in the attic of this 3-
story townhouse, and lots of the kids who go there
come down here afterward to hang out. Try the opium
drink – it's light and sweet. Creative cocktails – tasty
and strong.

SEYMOUR'S PARLOUR
ZETTER TOWNHOUSE
28-30 Seymour St, London, 020 7324 4555
www.thezettertownhouse.com
NEIGHBORHOOD: Marylebone
This is the intimate drawing room to Wicked Uncle Seymour, decorated with curious collections and antiques. Located in the Zetter Townhouse, a 24-bedroom Georgian townhouse, this unique cocktail lounge offers a unique cocktail experience. Private rooftop terrace.

TERROIRS
5 William IV St, London, +44 20 7036 0660
www.terroirswinebar.com

NEIGHBORHOOD: Covent Garden, Strand
Cute little cozy French wine bar. If you get hungry they have a small menu of tapas-style plates and a couple of desserts. Huge selection of wines.

THE WHIP
Mayfair Hotel
1st Floor, 50 Davies St, +44 20 7493 1275
www.thewhipmayfair.co.uk/
WEBSITE DOWN AT PRESSTIME
NEIGHBORHOOD: Mayfair
Located above The Running Horse in the Mayfair Hotel, known as Mayfair's coziest cocktail bar that pulls in the wealthy Mayfair set. This speakeasy style, Kentucky Derby themed cocktail bar with its racing green striped walls is a treat. Lots of race track stuff adorn the walls (riding crops, etc.). The bartenders are pros, so you can get proper American cocktails expertly prepared. Food is Southern style bar bites.

INDEX

1

10 GREEK STREET, 19

2

214 BERMONDSEY, 97

A

African (West Africa), 60
Afternoon Tea, 56, 83
ALAIN DUCASSE, 20
American, 41
ANCHOR & HOPE, 21
ANGLER, 23
Anglo-Indian, 64

Asian inspired, 76
AULIS, 24

B

Bakery, 29
BAO FITZROVIA, 25
BAR ITALIA, 98
BARBARY, 26
BARRAFINA, 28
BEA'S OF BLOOMSBURY, 29
BENARES, 29
BIBENDUM, 36
Bistro, 47
BLACK AXE MANGAL, 30
BLIND PIG, 98
BLIND SPOT, 98
BOOKING OFFICE BAR, 99
BRIGHT, 31
British, 37, 40, 76, 82, 89
British cuisine, 44
British (Modern), 23, 84
British cuisine, 22, 24, 33, 35,
    39, 43, 45, 46, 49, 57, 59,
    63
BUBBLEDOGS, 32
BUSES, 11
BY BICYCLE, 12
BY CAR, 12

C

**CADENHEAD'S WHISKEY
    SHOP**, 100
CAT & MUTTON, 33, 100
CEVICHE PERUVIAN KITCHEN,
    34
Champagne Bar, 32
CHILTERN FIREHOUSE, 34
Chinese, 53
CLAUDE BOSI, 36

CLOVE CLUB, 37
Coburg Bar,, 56
CONNAUGHT, 55
Connaught Bar, 56
Connaught Grill, 56
CORA PEARL, 39
CORAL ROOM, 35
CORE BY CLAIRE SMYTH, 40
CRAFT LONDON, 101
CRAZY COQS, 101
CUT, 41

D

DARJEELING EXPRESS, 42
DEAN STREET TOWNHOUSE,
    43
DELAUNAY, 44
**DINNER BY HESTON
    BLUMENTHAL**, 45
DORCHESTER, 20
DRAPERS ARMS, 46
DUCK & WAFFLE, 101
DUKE, 46

E

E. PELLICI, 47
EDWINS, 47
European, 24, 34, 39, 40, 85,
    89
European (Modern), 82
European (Modern), 58

F

Fish & Chips, 48
French, 40
French - Haute, 51, 55
French (Modern), 20, 36

FRYER'S DELIGHT, 48

G

GAME BIRD, 49
GETTING TO AND FROM THE AIRPORT, 14
GLORIA, 50
GREENHOUSE, 51
GYMKHANA, 52

H

HAKKASAN, 53
HAVELOCK TAVERN, 53
HAWKSMOOR, 54
HEATHROW AIRPORT, 14
HÉLÈNE DARROZE, 55
HEREFORD ROAD, 57
HIDE ABOVE, 58
HIX SOHO, 59
Hot Dogs, 32

I

IKOYI, 60
Indian, 29, 42, 52, 64
Italian, 31, 47, 50, 69, 75
Italian., 65
IVY, 60

J

Jean-Georges, 56
JOSE, 61

K

KILN, 62

Kitchen Table, 33
KITTY FISHER'S WOOD GRILL, 63
KRICKET, 64

L

LA BODEGA NEGRA, 64
LA FAMIGLIA, 65
LA GAVOCHE, 66
LE MANOIR AUX QUAF'SAISONS, 67
LEDBURY, 66
LOCANDA LOCATELLI, 68
LYLE'S, 69

M

MARK'S BAR, 102
MEATLIQUOR, 70
Mediterranean, 26, 54, 73
Mexican, 65
Middle Eastern, 26
MILK, 70
MINICABS, 10
Modern European, 20, 31, 44, 61
MONOCLE CAFÉ, 71
MOTORBIKES AND SCOOTERS, 13

N

NEPTUNE, 72

O

OPIUM, 103
OTTOLENGHI, 73

Oyster Card, 8

P

PADELLA, 75
PALOMAR, 76
Peruvian, 34
PIDGIN, 76
PIZARRO, 77
Pizza, 54
POLLEN STREET SOCIAL, 78

Q

QUO VADIS, 79

R

RABOT 1745, 79
RANDALL & AUBIN, 80
**Restaurant Terrace at the
     Ritz**, 82
RIDING HOUSE CAFÉ, 81
RITZ, 82
ROCHELLE CANTEEN, 85
ROGANIC, 84

S

SALON, 85
SCOTT'S, 86
Secret Garden Bar, 83
SEXY FISH, 87
SEYMOUR'S PARLOUR, 104
SMOKEHOUSE, 88
Social Eating House, 98
SOIF, 88

Somerset House, 89
Spanish, 28, 61
SPRING, 89
ST JOHN, 90
Stafford, The, 49
Steakhouse, 41, 54
STORY, 80
SWEETINGS FISH, 90

T

Taiwanese, 25
Tapas Bars, 61
TAXIS, 9
TERROIRS, 91, 104
Thai, 62
TRAMSHED, 92
Travelcard, 8
Turkish, 30

U

UNDERGROUND, 7

W

WHIP, 105
WILTONS, 93
WOLSELEY, 94
**WRIGHT BROTHERS OYSTER
     & PORTER HOUSE**, 95

Z

ZETTER TOWNHOUSE, 104

WANT 3 **FREE** THRILLERS?

Why, of course you do!
If you like these writers--
Vince Flynn, Brad Thor, Tom Clancy, James Patterson, David Baldacci, John Grisham, Brad Meltzer, Daniel Silva, Don DeLillo
If you like these TV series –
House of Cards, Scandal, West Wing, The Good Wife, Madam Secretary, Designated Survivor

---

You'll love the **unputdownable** series about
Jack Houston St. Clair, with political intrigue, romance, and loads of action and suspense.

Besides writing travel books, I've written political thrillers for many years that have delighted hundreds of thousands of readers. I want to introduce you to my work!
Send me an email and I'll send you a link where you can download the first 3 books in my bestselling series, absolutely FREE.
Mention **this book** when you email me.
andrewdelaplaine@mac.com

CPSIA information can be obtained
at www.ICGtesting.com
Printed in the USA
FSHW021532121021
85414FS

9 781393 855873